A Society &
Kew Gardens

A Society & Kew Gardens

Level 600 Reader (L+)
(CERF B1)

Virginia Woolf

Emily Aitken (Adaptor)
John McLean (Series Editor)

MATATABI PRESS

VIRGINIA WOOLF

Virginia Woolf
1882 - 1941

Adeline Virginia Woolf was a well-known UK writer born into a wealthy and influential family in London on January 25th, 1882. Her father, Sir Leslie Stephen, was a renowned writer and editor. During her childhood, she met famous British writers and poets like Henry James, George Eliot (Mary Ann Evans), and Alfred Tennyson.

Virginia's literature focuses on gender, class, and mental health. Her unique writing style, using a technique called "stream-of-consciousness narration," allows readers to see her characters' thoughts and emotions. Examples of this technique can be found in her well-known works, such as "Mrs. Dalloway" and "To the Lighthouse."

Virginia was known for her intelligence and her willingness to challenge societal norms, particularly those related to gender and sexuality. Tragically, she suffered from mental health issues and was severely depressed throughout her life. Virginia ultimately passed away by suicide in 1941. However, her writing and feminist ideologies have remained relevant, serving as an inspiration to many for more than a century.

Copyright © 2023 by MATATABI PRESS (910554), a subdivision of MATATABI HOLDINGS

All rights reserved. No part of this book may be reproduced in any manner whatsoever without written permission except in the case of brief quotations embodied in critical articles and reviews.

First Printing, March 2023

MATATABI PRESS (910554)
Windwhistle, Farley Hill, Matlock. DE4 3LL. UK
20-20, 5-Chome, Yamamoto-shinmachi, Asaminami-ku, Hiroshima.
731-0139. JAPAN
https://www.press.matatabi-japan.com/
https://www.holdings.matatabi-japan.com/
Email: press@matatabi-japan.com
Tel: 0081-(0)70-8592-2501

ACKNOWLEDGEMENTS

Special thanks are due to the students of the Department of English at Yasuda Women's University in Hiroshima, Japan, who played a crucial role in the final editing stages. They painstakingly reviewed the two stories in this book, ensuring that it is well-suited for EFL and ESL students around the world. Their diligence and commitment to excellence have greatly contributed to the quality of this book.

CONTENTS

VIRGINIA WOOLF   v
ACKNOWLEDGEMENTS   ix

PART 1: A SOCIETY

1. THE BEGINNING   2
2. CAPTAINS & JUDGES   9
3. ARTISTS & PROFESSORS   15
4. WHAT IS PURITY?   21
5. REGAINING FOCUS   28
6. LITERATURE &...   33

CONTENTS

7	THE WAR IS OVER	40

PART 2: KEW GARDENS

8	DRAGONFLIES	48
9	PURPLE BLACK DRESS	52
10	TWO ELDERLY WOMEN	56
11	YOUNG LOVE	59

A SOCIETY: VOCABULARY	67
A SOCIETY: ANSWERS	83
KEW GARDENS: VOCABULARY	95
KEW GARDENS: ANSWERS	101
NOTE FROM THE PUBLISHER	105
EDITORS	111

PART 1: A SOCIETY

1

THE BEGINNING

This is how our *society* began. One day, I was in a London teashop with some friends. After drinking tea, we sat around an open fire. As usual, we talked about men. We talked about how strong, brave, and intelligent they are.

"They have such good manners, and they're *so* handsome," one of us said.

"If I had a husband, my life would be perfect!" another said.

Polly listened quietly without saying a word. Suddenly, she covered her eyes with her hands and cried so hard that her whole body shook.

Before I continue, let me tell you about Polly.

We all love Polly, but she's a little strange. Her father was strange, too. He was also very, very rich. When he died, he left all of his money to Polly. However, there was one condition. She had to read every book in the London Library. We all knew it was impossible, but we didn't tell her.

Books and Stationery [1]

After some time, Polly stopped crying. "Every day for the last few months," she said, "I've gone to the London Library." We nodded. "First, I read all of the books listed under English literature. Then, I started to read books listed under biography, history, and gardening. Yesterday, a terrible thing happened… I cannot read another book." She stood up. "Most books," she yelled, "are page after page after page of nonsense!"

We didn't believe her. "What about Shakespeare, Milton and Shelley?" we yelled.

"Oh, yes," Polly said. "Shakespeare's plays are excellent. Milton's poems are wonderful, and Shelley's essays, fiction and drama are superb, but the others…"

Polly wiped the tears from her eyes. She picked up a book, *In a Garden* by Benton. She read the first few pages. We listened in silence.

"Yes, it's nonsense, but that's not a book," one of us said.

Polly picked up another book. It was a history book. We became excited. She started to read.

"That's not true! That didn't happen!" we yelled. Polly closed the book.

"Poetry! Poetry!" we said excitedly. "Read us some poetry!"

Polly picked up a small book of poetry. She put one hand on her chest and started to read. We were shocked. It really was word after word of nonsense.

"It must have been written by a woman," one of us said.

"It must have been written by an amateur," another said.

No, the author was a man, and he was not an amateur. He was one of Britain's most famous poets.

Polly picked up another book, *The Private Lives of Government Leaders*. "No more, Polly," we yelled. "Please, no more." She opened the book and started to read.

When Polly had finished reading, Jane, the eldest and most intelligent among us, stood up. "I don't believe you, Polly," she said. "If men write nonsense, why do women waste their youth giving birth to babies?"

We all silently thought about what Jane had said. "Why? Why did my father teach me to read?" Polly said, crying.

Clorinda breathed in deeply. "We women are at fault," she said. "All of us here can read, but only Polly has spent time reading. Up to now, I believed that women should spend their youth giving birth to children. My mother gave birth to ten children, and my grandmother, fifteen. I always dreamed of having twenty. I believed that all men were intelligent and hard working. I believed that all men were knowledgeable and that the books they wrote and pictures they drew improved the world." She looked around the room. "We can all read," she said, raising her fist. "It's time for us women to look closely at the world men have created."

Everybody agreed. We would go out into the world and ask question after question until we understood what this world men had created was really like. We would read books, go to museums and art galleries, go to concerts, and even watch people in the streets. We would not stop until we could answer the question:

- Does society produce *good people* and *good books*?

What's more, we would all remain pure until this question had been answered. No one would enter into a relationship with a man or give birth to a baby until we were satisfied.

QUIZ 1.1

1. Where did the *society* begin?
2. What was everybody talking about while sitting around the open fire?
3. Describe Polly's father?
4. What did Polly's father leave for Polly when he died?
5. What did Polly have to do to get it? Do you think it's possible? Why? / Why not?
6. What has Polly done every day for the last few months?
7. What terrible thing happened to her? Why?
8. What does Polly think about Shakespeare (1582 - 1616)?
9. How many of the following plays by Shakespeare do you know?
    i. The Merchant of Venice
    ii. Romeo and Juliet
    iii. The Tempest
    iv. Twelfth Night
    v. Othello

vi. King Lear
   vii. Much Ado About Nothing
   viii. Midsummer Night's Dream
   ix. Macbeth
   x. Hamlet
10. What does Polly think about Milton (1608 - 1674) and Shelley (1792 - 1822)?
11. What did everybody say about the poetry that Polly read?
12. Polly said, "Why did my father teach me to read?" Why do you think she said this?
13. What does Clorinda think they are at fault for? Do you agree?
14. What question did they agree to answer?
15. What did they agree not to do?

2

CAPTAINS & JUDGES

Some of our members went to the British Museum. Some went to the King's Navy. Some went to Oxford University and others to Cambridge. Some visited the Royal Academy of Arts and the Tate Gallery. Some went to concerts, law courts, and theaters. Others dined with men. Everywhere we went, we asked questions. Then, at regular intervals, we held *society* meetings to share what we had learned.

The King's Navy [2]

Those meetings were fun! I laughed so much when Rose told us about her experience with the King's Navy. She dressed up as a North African prince and boarded a ship. Unfortunately, the crew soon realized that she was not a prince and locked her in a room. After some time, the captain arrived. He angrily kicked open the door. "You've humiliated the King's Navy," he yelled. "Prepare to be punished!"

"Punished? Why?" Rose asked nervously.

"To restore the honor of the King's Navy, of course," he said, raising a long, hard stick above his head.

Fearing death, Rose bent over, stuck out her bottom, and waited to be hit. To her surprise, however, the captain did not hit her. Far from it, he gently tapped her bottom six times with the stick.

"Is that it?" Rose asked.

"Yes!" the captain replied calmly. "The honor of the King's Navy is satisfied."

"But my honor is not satisfied," she said, bending over again. "Hit me again, Captain!"

"Good man," the captain said. "Now, how many times should I hit you to satisfy your honor? Tell me about yourself."

Rose talked about her family and childhood. The captain smiled and laughed as he listened. When she had finished, the captain once again picked up his stick, and Rose once again bent over. "You're a good man," the captain said. "Your honor will be satisfied if I hit you four more times."

After that, the captain took Rose to a restaurant. They drank two bottles of wine together and promised to be best friends forever.

Next, let me tell you about Fanny's experience in a court of law. After her first visit, she concluded that judges were not human. "Judges," she said, "are large animals trained to nod their heads and make sounds that nobody can understand."

Law Court Judge [3]

On Fanny's second visit, she decided to test her idea that judges were animals. She carried a bagful of flies into the court of law and opened it. The flies happily buzzed around above everybody's heads. Unfortunately, the buzzing sound was so pleasant that Fanny soon fell asleep. When she finally woke up, the trial had finished and the prisoners were being led out of the courthouse. All the same, based on her description, we agreed that judges were animals, not men.

QUIZ 1.2

1. List five different locations that *society* members visited.
2. What did the members do at each location they visited?
3. How often did the members meet, and what did they talk about?
4. Where did Rose go, and what did she wear?
5. What did the captain do to Rose? Why?
6. What did Rose ask the captain to do? Why?
7. What did the captain and Rose talk about?
8. What did the captain and Rose promise one another?
9. Where did Fanny go?
10. How does Fanny describe judges?
11. What did Fanny bring on her second visit?
12. What did she do with it?
13. Why did Fanny fall asleep?
14. What was happening when Fanny woke up?
15. What did the *society* members agree on?

3

ARTISTS & PROFESSORS

Helen went to the Royal Academy of Arts to learn about the paintings created by men. When it was her turn to share what she had learned, she stood up, opened a blue book from the Academy, and began to read... a poem:

Home is the hunter,
 home from the hill
...
Love is sweet,
 love is brief
...

VIRGINIA WOOLF

*Men must work and
women must weep.*

"Stop!" we yelled. "We don't want to hear poetry. Tell us about the paintings."

Helen turned to the next page. "Daughters of England!" she began.

"No!" we yelled, pulling at her arm.

"Help me!" she said, shaking. "I can't get this nonsense out of my head!"

"Okay, okay, just tell us how big most of the paintings were," we said. "That's all we need to know."

Helen gestured the size with her hands. Then, she sat down, breathed a long sigh of relief, and smiled.

Castalia was the next to speak. She had visited a university to find out if they produce *good people* and *good books*. She got into the professors' apartments and offices by dressing up as a cleaner.

"Professors," she said, standing up, "live in a strange world. In many ways, it's like a prison. Throughout the universities, there are beautiful grass gardens. Around these gardens stand old stone buildings that the professors live and work in. Their apartments and offices are filled from floor to ceiling with books and research papers. There are no children, and, except for a few stray cats, no animals."

"Did you read any of the books or papers?" we asked excitedly.

"Well," she continued, "I found an interesting book about Sappho, the ancient Greek poet. It was in Professor Hobkin's office. He'd written it with a professor from Germany. It was hundreds of pages long."

"Sappho, the female poet?" we asked, moving closer to listen. "What did he say about her poetry?"

"Nothing," Helen replied, "nothing at all, it wasn't about her poetry. It was about her purity. The German professor claimed that she was impure, and Professor Hobkin claimed that she was not. While reading it, I kept thinking, *What does Professor Hobkin know about purity?*"

Sappho (Right) [4]

We misunderstood her.

"No! No!" she yelled. "He's a very nice, honorable old gentleman, but I can't image he's ever been with a woman."

We misunderstood her again.

"I'm sure he's never been with a man either," she said.

"So, what about universities?" one of us asked. "Do they?" one of us asked.

"Do they what?" Castalia replied.

"Do they produce *good people* and *good books*?" we all shouted.

"Oh! I forgot about that," Castalia replied. "I'll go back and find out."

QUIZ 1.3

1. Why did Helen go to the Royal Academy of Arts?
2. What was in the blue book that Helen read?
3. Why do you think Helen was shaking?
4. How did Helen describe the paintings?
5. Why did Castalia go to a university?
6. How did Castalia get into the professors' apartments and offices?
7. Why do you think Castalia said the professors lived in a world similar to a prison?
8. Describe the professors' apartments and offices.
9. Who wrote the book that Castalia read?
10. What was the book about?
11. Why do you think Castalia said, "What does Professor Hobkin know about purity?"?
12. Why did Castalia say she would return to the university?

4

WHAT IS PURITY?

The next time I saw Castalia was three months later at a *society* meeting. When she entered the room, she looked... special. Everything about her was beautiful; the way she walked, the expression on her face, and even her mood. I ran across the room and hugged her.

"I went back to the university," Castalia said.

"Asking questions?" I asked.

"Finding answers," she replied.

"Do you remember what we agreed?" I asked, looking at her stomach.

"Oh, that," Castalia said, smiling. "Staying pure

until we understand what this world men have created is really like."

I nodded.

"I met someone at the university," she casually said. "We're going to have a baby. It's so exciting, so beautiful, so satisfying—."

"What is?" I asked.

"Answering the questions, of course," she replied shyly, changing the topic. Castalia told me about everything that had happened during her visits to the university.

"But, what about our agreement?" I asked.

"If you really cared about purity, you wouldn't have hugged me," Castalia said. "I know that you're just as impure as I am."

"True!" I replied, hugging her again.

The other *society* members started entering the room. Their eyes shone with delight when they saw Castalia. They kissed her and said how happy they were to see her again.

After everybody had arrived, Jane stood up. "We've been asking questions for five years now," she said, "and our results are inconclusive. We still don't know if this world that men have created produces *good people* and *good books*. However—"

Castalia raised her hand. "Before you say any more, I want to ask if I can stay in the room." She stood up. "I'm an impure woman. I broke our agreement."

Everybody looked at her in surprise.

"Are you going to have a baby?" Jane asked.

Castalia nodded.

Jane looked around the room. "What do you think?" she asked. "Should we ask her to leave? Is she impure?"

"No! No! No!" we all yelled so loudly that passersby on the street outside could hear us. "Let her stay! She's not impure! That's nonsense!"

One of our youngest members raised her hand. "What is purity? Is it good? Is it bad, or is it nothing at all?" she asked nervously.

Polly stood up. She looked tired from spending day after day in the London Library. "Purity," she said, "is simply a lack of knowledge and experience. It is wrong to describe a woman as pure or impure. Some of us here don't have the opportunity to be impure."

"My baby's father is twenty-one. He's very handsome," Castalia said joyfully, lost in her thoughts.

Helen stood up. "I want to recommend a new rule," she said. "No one can talk about purity or impurity unless she is in love."

"Oh, that's too bad," said Judith, who had been asking questions to scientists. "I'm not in love, but I want to talk about impurity. I've had a great idea. London has a problem with sex workers. I know how to both solve that problem and help single women get pregnant." She held up a map of the London Underground. "In each subway station," Judith said, pointing at the map, "we need to build a special room. Men can visit these rooms to deposit sperm. The sperm of government leaders, poets, painters, musicians, and so on can be kept in glass tubes. Then, women who want to get pregnant can visit these rooms to select the sperm they want." She looked around the room. "Do women still want to give birth?" she asked.

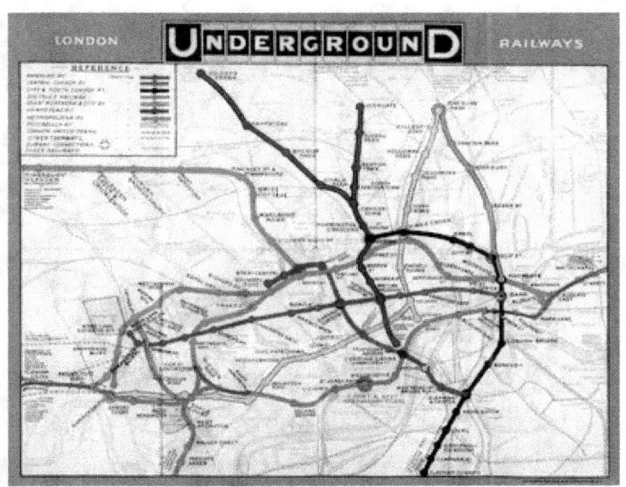

London Underground 1908 [5]

"Of course we want to give birth!" Castalia yelled.

"Silence, everybody," Jane said, tapping on the table. "Judith has raised a very good question. *Do women still want to give birth?* As a society, we've been asking ourselves this question for five years now. Castalia has expressed her opinion. She thinks that it's okay to bring more children into this world. Now, the rest of us decide whether bringing more children into this world is acceptable."

QUIZ 1.4

1. When and where did the narrator next see Castalia?
2. In what ways did Castalia look beautiful?
3. Where had Castalia been and why?
4. What did Castalia say was so exciting, so beautiful, and so satisfying?
5. What had the *society* members agreed to do?
6. Why do you think the *society* members' eyes shined with delight when they saw Castalia?
7. How many years have passed since the first *society* meeting?
8. What do the *society* members think is nonsense? Do you agree? Why? / Why not?
9. How does Polly define *purity*?
10. How do you think Castalia met her partner?
11. What kind of men had Judith been talking to?
12. At the time of this story, England was a class society (upper class, middle class, and working class). What class of men do you think

Judith wanted to visit the special rooms in the underground?
13. What class or type of women do you think Judith expected to work in the special rooms?
14. What class or type of women do you think Judith expected to visit the special rooms as customers?
15. What did Jane say the other members of the *society* must now decide?

5

REGAINING FOCUS

Science and engineering were the next topics of discussion. Three *society* members stood up, one after another, to tell us what they had learned. Needless to say, we were amazed. Man's scientific and engineering achievements were far better than any of us imagined. We learned how airplanes fly, how telephones work, and how scientists look into the atom. Following these discussions, everybody agreed that our mothers were right to give up their youth to give birth to such men. Castalia was delighted.

A SOCIETY & KEW GARDENS

Nieuport Airplane [6]

In the next session, we learned how many people live in England, what percentage is hungry in prison, how many children the average working woman gives birth to, and how many women die from problems connected to childbirth. Some members talked about factories, shops, poor neighborhoods, and ships. Others talked about the Stock Exchange, the huge houses where business leaders meet, government offices, and British rule in India, Africa and Ireland.

I was sitting next to Castalia. She looked unhappy. "We'll never reach a conclusion if we continue like this," she said. "The world is far too complex. We need to focus on our original question: *Does society produce good people and good books?*"

Castalia was right. Talking about atoms, airplanes, and the Stock Exchange was not helping us reach a conclusion. It was time to regain focus. We needed to talk about men. Everybody agreed.

One by one, members placed their answers to the complex questions we had been asking on a table in the middle of the room. When everybody had returned to her seat, Jane stood up. "A *good man*," she said, "must be honest and passionate. He must be interested in more than money, power, and goods. To find out if a man has these qualities, we must be wise. We cannot simply ask a man if he is honest or passionate. We need to be indirect. We need to ask questions such as:

i. Where is your son—and *daughter*—being educated?

ii. How much do you pay for your cigars?

iii. Why do you work 15 hours a day?

Jane formally closed the meeting. We all went home with renewed hope of reaching a conclusion.

QUIZ 1.5

1. What were the first two topics the *society* members discussed?
2. How many members talked about those topics?
3. What did the members think about man's achievements in those fields?
4. What recent achievements in those fields interest you? Why?
5. Why do you think Castalia was delighted?
6. Members learned how many people live in England, i.e. its population.
   i. What was the population of your country in 1914?
   ii. What is the population of your country now?
7. Members learned what percentage of the population in England is hungry in prison. What percentage of your country's population is in prison?
8. Members learned how many children the

average working woman in England gives birth to. How many children does the average woman give birth to in your country?

9. Members learned how many women in England die from problems connected to childbirth. How many women die from problems connected to childbirth in your country?
10. Why did Castalia look unhappy?
11. What did the members do with their answers to the complex questions they had been asking?
12. What character trait do you think each of the following questions reveals?
    i. Where is your son—and *daughter*—being educated?
    ii. How much do you pay for your cigars?
    iii. Why do you work 15 hours a day?

6

LITERATURE &...

Getting men to answer our new questions was more challenging than we had expected. Most men refused to talk about religion or what it meant to be good. What's more, when we asked about the meaning of money or power, many ignored us or became angry. I'm sure that the only reason none of us were attacked was because some men think that women are below them.

"Of course, they think we are below them,' Eleanor said, opening a newspaper. 'That's what the newspapers tell them. Listen to what this journalist has written: *There have been no first-rate women writers or poets since Sappho.*"

"What about Jane Austen, Charlotte Brontë, and George Eliot?" Polly yelled. "They were all first-rate writers."

"Yes, I agree. They *were*," Eleanor replied. "However, is there a woman alive today who can write like a first-rate man?"

"Elizabeth," Jane called out, "you've been researching literature. Tell us what you have learned."

Elizabeth walked to the middle of the room. "As you know," she said, "for the last five years, I've been dressing up as a man and pretending to be an editor. I've become close to many of England's best-known writers. Mr. H. G. Wells is the most popular writer alive today. The second most popular is Mr. Arnold Bennett, then Mr. Compton Mackenzie, Mr. Stephen McKenna, and Mr. Hugh Walpole." Without saying another word, Elizabeth sat down.

"But you haven't told us anything about their writing!" we yelled. "Are these men better writers than Austen, Brontë, and Eliot? Is the future of literature safe with these men?"

"Oh, yes. It's safe, very safe," Elizabeth said,

nervously moving from one foot to the other. "They're all very *good men*."

"Yes, maybe they are *good men*," we said, "but do they write *good books*?"

"*Good books*?" she said, looking at the ceiling. "Well, many of their books describe real life. One book I read, for example, has a lot of useful information about where to stay in Brighton. Another book has information about what you can do on a raining Sunday evening."

"What does that have to do with being a *good book*?" we asked.

"Nothing, nothing, nothing at all," she replied.

"Tell us the truth," we demanded. "Are the books these men write *good*?"

"The truth," Elizabeth said, returning to her seat, "has nothing to do with literature."

Jane stood up again. "Ladies," she began, "we must try to agree—"

"War! War! War! England is at war!" Men were shouting in the street outside.

We looked at each other in shock.

"What war?" we yelled. "What war?"

VIRGINIA WOOLF

Britain Declares War on Germany [7]

Polly had read a number of history books in the London Library. "Why do men go to war?" we asked.

"Sometimes for one reason, and sometimes for another," she replied. "In 1760, for example, England went to war for one reason. In 1797, it went to war for another. Then, in 1804, it went to war for yet another reason. In 1866, the Prussians fought the Austrians for control of Germany. Then, in 1870—"

"But it's 1914!" we yelled. "Why are we going to war now?"

"Ah, I don't know," she replied.

QUIZ 1.6

1. What topics did most men refuse to talk about?
2. What topics do people in your country prefer not to talk about?
3. How did men react when *society* members asked them about money or power?
4. Why does the narrator think no one was attacked when asking these questions?
5. Why do many men think that women are below them?
6. What three famous women writers does Polly mention?
7. What had Elizabeth been researching?
8. What did she pretend to be?
9. Who does Elizabeth say is the second most popular writer?
10. What does Elizabeth say the five men write about?
11. What does Elizabeth say has nothing to do

with literature? Do you agree? Why? / Why not?
12. Jane said, "Ladies, we must try to agree—" What do you think she was going to say?
13. What were the men in the street shouting?
14. Why did the Prussians go to war with the Austrians?
15. What do people in your country call the war that started in 1914?

7

THE WAR IS OVER

The war was over. A peace agreement was being discussed. Castalia and I were in the room where, before the war, we had held our *society* meetings. We were reading the notes we had taken at our meetings.

"It's strange. I can't believe we were so naive five years ago," I said, looking at the notes.

"Definitely," Castalia said, leaning over my shoulder. She read a line from one of the notes: "*The objective of life is to produce good people and good books... A good man is honest, passionate, and interested in more than money, power, and goods.*"

"We wrote like women!" I said.

"We were so foolish!" Castalia said. A look of anger spread across her face. "If we hadn't learned to read," she said, "we would all be happy like our mothers. We would be having babies and bringing up children now, believing that life could not be better."

"True, but it must have been hard for them. They had to watch their sons grow up and go to—" I started to say.

"War?" Castalia said, finishing my sentence. "Yes. They watched their sons grow up and watched them go to war to be killed. They couldn't read, and *they* didn't complain about the world. They were happy."

"How's your daughter?" I asked, changing the topic.

Castalia breathed in deeply and sighed. "I tried to stop her from learning to read," she said, "but it's impossible. Yesterday, I caught her looking at a newspaper. Soon, she'll be asking me if the Prime Minister, Mr. Lloyd George, is a good man. Then, she'll ask me if the author Mr. Arnold Bennett is a good writer. After that, she'll ask me if I believe in God."

"What's wrong with that?" I said.

"I want her to be happy," Castalia replied. "However, the only way that'll happen is if she believes in nothing."

"You could try to make her believe that men are more intelligent than women," I suggested, smiling ironically.

Castalia laughed. "Cassy," she said, "that's the biggest lie that has ever been told."

"Really?" I said, laughing. "If you ask any journalist, school teacher, politician or even pub owner in England, they will tell you that men are more intelligent than women."

"Of course they will," Castalia replied. "For thousands of years, mothers have been helping their sons grow and learn. Mothers have always wanted their sons to be intelligent. When boys first start learning, they're so beautiful. They love life. They love art. They love literature, and they don't look down on anybody. Then, their intelligence becomes focused. They become lawyers, civil servants, writers, or professors. They use their intelligence to support their family. That's when the problems start. That's when they start to look down on women." Castalia sighed. "Cassy," she said, looking at me, "let's find a way for men to get pregnant and give birth. They need an innocent occupation. That's the only way for them to be *good people* and to write *good books*. It's the only way to stop them from using their intelligence to destroy the world. If they continue like this, no one will be alive to know about Shakespeare!"

"It is too late," I replied. "The war they created took everything."

"Intelligence took everything," Castalia said.

Tired and exhausted men yelled in the street outside. *A Peace Treaty has been signed.* Their voices became quiet. It started to rain.

"I must go home," Castalia said. "My cook always puts the evening newspaper on the dinner table. I need to stop my daughter, Ann, from trying to read it."

"She's going to learn how to read," I said. "There's only one thing you can teach her to believe in."

"What's that?" Castalia asked.

"Herself. Teach her to believe in herself," I said.

We picked up our *society's* notes and went to

Castalia's house. Ann was happily playing with her toys. We gave her the notes. "Ann, you're the new and future president of our *society*," we said together. She took the notes and burst into tears.

QUIZ 1.7

1. What was being discussed and between which four countries (research)?
2. Where were the narrator and Castalia?
3. What did the narrator feel was strange?
4. What did *society* members think the objective of life was?
5. What qualities did the *society* members say a good man must have? Do you agree?
6. Why did a look of anger spread across Castalia's face?
7. Why does Castalia think her mother was happy?
8. What did Castalia try to stop her daughter from doing?
9. Who was Mr. Lloyd George?
10. Why does the narrator smile ironically when she says that Castalia should try to make her daughter believe that men are more intelligent than women?
11. What is the narrator's name?

12. In 1921, when this story was first published, most journalists, school teachers, politicians, and pub owners in England were men.
    i. What was the situation like in your country in 1921?
    ii. How about now?
13. What does Castalia say mothers have been doing for their sons for thousands of years?
14. What does Castalia say men need to do to be *good people* and to write *good books*?
15. What does the narrator say Castalia should teach her daughter, Ann?

PART 2: KEW GARDENS

8

DRAGONFLIES

Kew Gardens in south-west London has gardens containing plants from all over the world. In the center of one of the gardens, there is an oval-shaped flowerbed with over a hundred flowers, each with heart-shaped leaves and colorful petals. It's July, and the gentle summer breeze moves the flowers from side to side. The sunlight highlights a snail's shell. Visitors walk from garden to garden.

A man approaches the flowerbed. He's thinking about a woman called Lily. *Fifteen years ago, I came here with Lily. We sat by that lake and I asked her to marry me. A dragonfly flew in circles above our heads. I knew she was going to say "No" by looking at her foot. She was moving it from side to side. However, I thought, 'If the dragonfly lands on her foot, she will stop moving it. Then, she will say "Yes."' Luckily, it didn't land on her foot, and she didn't say "Yes." If she had, I wouldn't be here with Eleanor and the kids.*

A woman was walking one-step behind the man. Two children were following her. The man looked at her. "Tell me, Eleanor," he said. "Do you ever think about the past?"

"Why do you ask, Simon?" she replied.

"Because I've been thinking about the past," he said. "I've been thinking about Lily. This is where I asked her to marry me."

The woman stopped in front of the flowerbed. She was silent.

The man walked toward her. "Do you dislike it when I think about the past?" he said.

"Of course not, Simon?" she said. "We all remember our past when we see young men and women sitting together under the trees."

"What do you remember, Eleanor?" the man asked.

Water Lilies [8]

"A kiss," she said, smiling. "I remember six young girls, sitting by that lake, painting pictures of water lilies. It was 20 years ago, and it was the first time I had ever seen a red water lily. Suddenly, someone kissed me on the back of my neck. My whole body shook with delight. My hands shook all afternoon. The kiss was from an old woman with gray hair. It was the most wonderful kiss I have ever experienced."

The man was silent.

The woman turned toward the children. "Come on, Caroline! Come on, Hubert," she called out.

The man, woman and children walked away from the flowerbed together. The sun shone on their backs as they disappeared into the distance.

QUIZ 2.1

1. Where is Kew Gardens and what can be found there?
2. What can be seen in the oval-shaped flowerbed in Kew Gardens?
3. What happened fifteen years ago when the man and Lily were at Kew Gardens?
4. What did the man imagine would happen if a dragonfly landed on Lily's foot?
5. Who was walking with the man and what did he ask her?
6. What does Eleanor remember about the kiss?
7. Who walked away from the flowerbed together?

9

PURPLE BLACK DRESS

The snail in the oval-shaped flowerbed started to move. It crawled over the loose earth. A strange insect passed in front of it. It stopped, but the snail did not. The snail had a goal, somewhere it needed to go. It moved closer and closer to insect. The insect thought for a moment. Then, it left in the opposite direction.

A SOCIETY & KEW GARDENS

Snail & Insect [9]

The snail had to get over several obstacles to reach its goal. The blades of grass were like trees to it. Stones were like huge rocks. Dead leaves were like big tents. Two men approached. They were upper-middle class. The younger man, William, was very calm. He looked straight ahead. The older man was impatient. He looked up toward the sky and spoke rapidly. He said that the ghosts of people who had died spoke to him. They told him strange things about Heaven. "William, Heaven used to be called Thessaly," he said. "This war that stated in 1914 is changing Heaven. There are too many widows, too many women in black."

The older man saw something in the distance. It was a woman in a purple black dress. He became excited and started waving at her. William grabbed his arm. "Look at this," he said, trying to calm him down. "Look at this beautiful flower."

The older man looked at the flower. Then, he turned his head to the side, put a hand behind his ear, and listened to it. He nodded and spoke to the flower. "Yes, I visited the beautiful forests of Uruguay hundreds of years ago," he said. "I went there with the most beautiful woman in Europe. We saw roses, nightingales, mermaids, and..." William gently pulled his arm, leading him away from the flowerbed.

QUIZ 2.2

1. What did the snail encounter as it moved towards its goal?
2. What was the strange insect's reaction to the snail's approach?
3. Who were the two men that approached the flower bed?
4. What did William do to calm the older man down?
5. What did the older man claim to have seen in Uruguay?

10

TWO ELDERLY WOMEN

Two elderly women, one overweight, the other red-cheeked and thin, followed closely behind the old man. They listened to him speak and watched him move. They weren't sure if he was eccentric or mad. They were lower-middle class and, like many lower-middle class people, they were interested in the lives of the upper-middle class.

After some time, they lost interest in the old man and returned to their conversation. They spoke energetically. "Nell, Bert, Phil, Father, he says, I says, she says, I says, I says, I says——" the overweight woman said.

"My Bert, Sister, Bill, Granddad, the old man, sugar, sugar, flour, greens, sugar, sugar, sugar," the thin woman replied.

The overweight woman stopped next to the oval-shaped flowerbed. She leaned over and looked at the flowers with curiosity. Her face looked like she had just woken up from a deep sleep. It looked like she was staring at the candlestick next to her bed. She ignored the thin woman who continued to talk to her. As she looked at the flowers, she slowly swayed backwards and forwards. Eventually, she stood up and said, "Come on! Let's go and have a cup of tea."

QUIZ 2.3

1. Who were the three people mentioned at the beginning of this chapter?
2. How did the elderly women feel about the old man?
3. What social class were the elderly women?
4. What were the elderly women interested in?
5. What did the overweight woman do when she stopped next to the oval-shaped flowerbed?
6. What did the overweight woman suggest to the thin woman?

11

YOUNG LOVE

The snail had thought of every possible way to reach its goal without going over or around a dead leaf. It didn't want to climb over the leaf because it was too difficult, and it would take a long time to go around it. Finally, it decided to go under it. As it passed under the leaf, two more people – a young couple on their first date – approached the oval-shaped flowerbed.

"Lucky it isn't Friday," the man said.

"Why?" the woman asked, looking confused.

"They make you pay ten percent extra on Fridays," the man said.

"Ten percent extra? It's worth it, isn't it?" the woman said.

"It? What do you mean by 'it'?" the man said, looking at the woman.

The couple silently pressed the end of the woman's parasol into the soft ground together. This action, as well as the fact that the man's hand rested on top of the woman's, showed their feelings for one another. Their words were short and insignificant, and didn't seem to have much meaning. They talked about having tea brought to them as they sat at a white table among the gardens. They talked about him paying the bill. It all felt like a dream to both of them. Just being together made them happy. The man pulled the parasol out of the ground. He wanted to find the ideal place for them to have tea together.

"Follow me, Trissie," he said to the woman. "It's time we had our tea."

"Where does everyone go to drink tea?" she asked, smiling widely, turning her head this way and that. However, she was too excited to think about tea. Her mind was full of everything she'd seen in Kew Gardens: beautiful orchids, cranes, wild flowers, a Chinese pagoda, and a bird with deep red-colored feathers on its head.

Wild Flowers [10]

One after another, people walked past the oval-shaped flowerbed. They moved in a strange and random way. As they walked, they disappeared into the colors of the gardens around them. At first, you could see their bodies and some color, but then everything disappeared. It was very hot. Even the songbirds stayed in the shade. White butterflies danced above the flowers. The glass roof of the palm tree house shone brightly. The sound of an airplane mixed with the sounds of people talking and laughing. People of all ages and colors were seen for a moment, and then they disappeared in the yellow and green atmosphere. Their voices filled the air, and the flowers continued to show their beautiful colors.

QUIZ 2.4

1. Why did the snail avoid going over or around the dead leaf?
2. Who approached the oval-shaped flowerbed as the snail passed under the leaf?
3. What did the man say about Fridays to the woman?
4. What did the couple talk about while they were together?
5. What was Trissie too excited to think about?
6. What did the man suggest Trissie do?
7. What did Trissie see at Kew Gardens?
8. What filled the air at Kew Gardens?

ILLUSTRATIONS

1. Books and Stationery: *Leo Gestel (ca. 1891 –1941)*
2. The King's Navy: *British Battleship HMS Anson (ca. 1897)*
3. Law Court Judge (Idle Lays of the Parliament House): *Howard Henderson (1882)*
4. Sappho (Right) (Sappho and Erinna in a Garden at Mytilene): *Simeon Solomon (1864)*
5. London Underground 1908: *Unknown Author*
6. Nieuport Airplane: *Claude Grahame White's Nieuport IV (ca. 1912)*
7. Britain Declares War on Germany: *Daily Mail issue Aug 5 1914*
8. Water Lilies: *Claude Monet* (1915–1926)
9. Snail & Insect: Adapted from *The Model*

ILLUSTRATIONS

Book of Calligraphy (1561–1596) *by Georg Bocskay and Joris Hoefnage*

10. Wild Flowers: *Monet's* Garden *in Giverny (1900) by Claude Monet*

A SOCIETY: VOCABULARY

NOUNS

1. *Academy*: a place of learning or an organization for the promotion of art, science, or culture
2. *Achievements*: accomplishments or successes in a particular area or field
3. *Agreement*: a mutual understanding or arrangement between two or more parties regarding a specific issue or matter
4. *Amateurs*: individuals who pursue a particular activity, usually in their spare time, without receiving payment or professional training
5. *Atom*: the basic unit of matter consisting of a nucleus of protons and neutrons, surrounded by electrons

A SOCIETY: VOCABULARY

6. *Author*: a person who writes books, articles, or other literary works
7. *Biography*: a written account of a person's life, often including information about their achievements and historical context
8. *British Museum*: a museum located in London that contains a vast collection of historical and cultural artifacts from around the world
9. *Captain*: a person in command of a ship, aircraft, or other vehicle
10. *Cigars*: a cylindrical roll of tobacco wrapped in tobacco leaves, typically smoked for pleasure
11. *Civil servants*: individuals who work for the government and are responsible for the implementation and administration of policies and programs
12. *Complex*: consisting of multiple interconnected parts or elements, often difficult to understand or analyze
13. *Conclusion*: a final decision or judgment reached after considering all available information

A SOCIETY: VOCABULARY

14. *Court*: a governmental or legal institution responsible for administering justice and resolving disputes
15. *Criteria*: standards or guidelines used to evaluate or assess something
16. *Delight*: a feeling of great pleasure or satisfaction
17. *Drama*: a literary genre that presents characters in conflict with each other or their surroundings, typically with intense emotions and tension
18. *Editor*: a person who prepares written works for publication, often by correcting or revising the content and style
19. *Essays*: a short piece of writing on a particular subject, often presenting the author's personal views or opinions
20. *Experience*: knowledge or skill acquired through involvement in a particular activity or exposure to a particular situation
21. *Fault*: a flaw or defect in something or someone
22. *Foolish*: lacking good sense or judgment; unwise or imprudent

A SOCIETY: VOCABULARY

23. *Galleries*: a building or room used for the exhibition or sale of works of art
24. *Gardening*: the practice of cultivating plants, often for food, ornamentation, or landscaping
25. *Government*: the system of institutions and individuals responsible for governing a country, state, or other political entity
26. *Impure*: containing impurities or contaminants; not clean or pure
27. *Impurity*: the state of being impure or contaminated
28. *Inconclusive*: not leading to a definite conclusion or outcome
29. *Information*: facts or knowledge about something or someone
30. *Intelligence*: the ability to learn, understand, and apply knowledge and skills
31. *Journalist*: A person who writes, reports, or broadcasts news stories for newspapers, magazines, television, or radio
32. *Literature*: Written works, especially those considered to have artistic or intellectual value, such as novels, poems, and plays

A SOCIETY: VOCABULARY

33. ***Nonsense***: Ideas, statements, or actions that lack sense or meaning
34. ***Navy***: The branch of a country's armed forces that is responsible for naval warfare and operations at sea
35. ***Objective***: Not influenced by personal feelings or opinions; based on facts and evidence
36. ***Occupation***: A person's job or profession
37. ***Painters***: People who create works of art using paint
38. ***Passionate***: Having or showing strong emotions or intense feelings about something
39. ***Peace Treaty***: An agreement between two or more countries or groups to end a war or conflict
40. ***Plays***: Performances of scripted dramas or comedies, usually in a theater
41. ***Poetry***: Literary works that use language to evoke emotion and express ideas, often using rhyme and meter
42. ***Poems***: Works of poetry that express emotions, ideas, or experiences through language and imagery
43. ***Prime Minister***: The head of the govern-

ment in a parliamentary democracy, typically appointed by the monarch or president

44. *Professors*: Teachers or scholars who teach at a college or university
45. *Prussia*: A former kingdom and state in central Europe, now part of modern-day Germany, Poland, and Russia
46. *Purity*: The state or quality of being pure or free from contaminants; someone who has never had a physical relationship
47. *Pub owner*: Someone who owns a public house that serves alcoholic beverages and sometimes food
48. *Religion*: A system of beliefs, values, and practices concerning the existence and nature of a higher power or powers
49. *Research papers*: Written works that present the findings of a specific research project or study
50. *Royal Academy of Arts*: A prestigious art institution in London, England, founded in 1768
51. *Society*: A group of people who share a common culture, values, and institutions

A SOCIETY: VOCABULARY

52. ***Stock Exchange***: A market where stocks and other securities are bought and sold
53. ***Tate Gallery***: A group of four art museums in the UK, including the Tate Britain, Tate Modern, Tate Liverpool, and Tate St Ives
54. ***Truth***: The quality or state of being in accordance with fact or reality
55. ***War***: A state of armed conflict between two or more nations or groups
56. ***Wise***: Having or showing good judgment, discernment, or understanding
57. ***Youth***: Young people, especially those between childhood and adulthood

VERBS

1. ***Achieve***: achieves, achieved, achieving - to successfully complete or accomplish a task or goal
2. ***Agree***: agrees, agreed, agreeing - to have the same opinion or to come to a consensus
3. ***Believe in***: believes in, believed in, believing in - to have faith or trust in something or someone

A SOCIETY: VOCABULARY

4. ***Begin***: begins, began, beginning - to start or initiate something
5. ***Breathe in***: breathes in, breathed in, breathing in - to inhale air into the lungs
6. ***Bring up***: brings up, brought up, bringing up - to raise a topic or subject for discussion
7. ***Buzz***: buzzes, buzzed, buzzing - to make a continuous, humming sound
8. ***Carry***: carries, carried, carrying - to transport or convey something from one place to another
9. ***Catch***: catches, caught, catching - to grasp or seize something in motion
10. ***Change***: changes, changed, changing - to make or become different
11. ***Claim***: claims, claimed, claiming - to assert or demand as one's own
12. ***Conclude***: concludes, concluded, concluding - to bring something to an end or arrive at a final decision
13. ***Connect***: connects, connected, connecting - to join or link together
14. ***Cry***: cries, cried, crying - to shed tears or make a wailing sound

A SOCIETY: VOCABULARY

15. *Declare*: declares, declared, declaring - to make a formal announcement or proclamation
16. *Decide*: decides, decided, deciding - to make a choice or reach a conclusion
17. *Describe*: describes, described, describing - to give an account or representation of something in words
18. *Demand*: demands, demanded, demanding - to ask for something forcefully or urgently
19. *Express*: expresses, expressed, expressing - to convey or communicate something in words, writing, or art
20. *Fall*: falls, fell, falling - to drop or descend from a higher to a lower position
21. *Fight*: fights, fought, fighting - to engage in physical combat or argue intensely
22. *Gesture*: gestures, gestured, gesturing - to make a movement or signal with the body or limbs
23. *Hold*: holds, held, holding - to have or keep in one's grasp or possession
24. *Humiliate*: humiliates, humiliated, humili-

A SOCIETY: VOCABULARY

ating - to cause someone to feel ashamed or embarrassed
25. *Ignore*: ignores, ignored, ignoring - to pay no attention to or disregard something or someone
26. *Laugh*: laughs, laughed, laughing - to express amusement or joy through sound and facial expression
27. *Lead*: leads, led, leading - to guide or direct a group or activity
28. *Misunderstand*: misunderstands, misunderstood, misunderstanding - to interpret something incorrectly or fail to comprehend it
29. *Observe*: observes, observed, observing - to watch or notice something carefully
30. *Pay*: pays, paid, paying - to give money in exchange for goods or services
31. *Pick up*: picks up, picked up, picking up - to lift or take something from a lower to a higher position
32. *Place*: places, placed, placing - to put or position something in a particular location

A SOCIETY: VOCABULARY

33. *Produce*: produces, produced, producing - to create or make something
34. *Raise*: raises, raised, raising - to lift or elevate something to a higher position
35. *Reach*: reaches, reached, reaching - to extend or stretch out to touch or grab something
36. *Recommend*: recommends, recommended, recommending - to suggest or endorse something for consideration or adoption
37. *Refuse*: refuses, refused, refusing - to decline to accept or comply with something
38. *Regain*: regains, regained, regaining - to recover or retrieve something that was lost or taken away
39. *Remain*: remains, remained, remaining - to continue to exist or stay in the same place or state
40. *Reply*: replies, replied, replying - to respond to someone or something by speaking or writing
41. *Restore*: restores, restored, restoring - to bring something back to its original or previous condition
42. *Shake*: shakes, shook, shaking - to move

back and forth or up and down quickly and repeatedly
43. *Shout*: shouts, shouted, shouting - to speak or cry out loudly, often in anger or excitement
44. *Sigh*: sighs, sighed, sighing - to breathe out audibly in a way that expresses sadness, relief, or tiredness
45. *Spread*: spreads, spread, spreading - to extend or distribute something over a surface or area
46. *Start*: starts, started, starting - to begin or commence something
47. *Stand*: stands, stood, standing - to be in an upright position on one's feet
48. *Stand up*: stands up, stood up, standing up - to rise to a standing position from a seated or lying position
49. *Visit*: visits, visited, visiting - to go or come to see someone or something
50. *Weep*: weeps, wept, weeping - to shed tears, usually as an expression of sorrow or grief
51. *Wipe*: wipes, wiped, wiping - to clean or

dry something by rubbing its surface with a cloth or one's hand
52. *Yell*: yells, yelled, yelling - to shout or scream loudly, often in anger or fear

ADJECTIVES

1. *Alive*: having life or living; not dead
2. *Ancient*: belonging to the very distant past and no longer in existence
3. *Brave*: ready to face and endure danger or pain; showing courage
4. *Challenging*: testing one's abilities or resources in a demanding but stimulating undertaking
5. *Delightful*: highly pleasing, especially to the senses; enjoyable
6. *Exhausted*: completely drained of energy; extremely tired
7. *First-rate*: of the highest quality or excellence
8. *Foolish*: lacking good sense or judgment; unwise

A SOCIETY: VOCABULARY

9. *Handsome*: pleasing in appearance; attractive
10. *Honorable*: deserving of respect and admiration; morally upright and principled
11. *Humiliated*: made to feel ashamed or foolish by injuring one's dignity or self-respect
12. *Impure*: not clean or wholesome; morally corrupt
13. *Interesting*: arousing curiosity or interest; engaging
14. *Intelligent*: having the ability to acquire and apply knowledge and skills; mentally sharp or clever
15. *Inconclusive*: not leading to a firm conclusion; not decisive
16. *Ironic*: using language that normally signifies the opposite, typically for humorous or emphatic effect
17. *Naïve*: lacking experience, wisdom, or judgment; unsophisticated
18. *Passionate*: having or showing strong feelings of enthusiasm or excitement
19. *Popular*: liked or admired by many people or by a particular group

A SOCIETY: VOCABULARY

20. *Pure*: not mixed or contaminated with any other substance; morally clean or virtuous
21. *Renewed*: restored to a fresh or new condition; revived
22. *Satisfying*: providing fulfillment or gratification; meeting one's expectations or desires
23. *Shocking*: causing a feeling of surprise or disbelief; outrageous
24. *Shy*: timid or reserved in the presence of others; lacking confidence
25. *Special*: unique or distinct in some way; exceptional
26. *Specific*: clearly defined or identified; relating to a particular thing
27. *Strange*: unusual or unfamiliar in appearance, behavior, or character
28. *Terrible*: extremely bad or unpleasant; causing terror or horror
29. *Tired*: in need of rest or sleep; exhausted
30. *Useful*: able to be used for a practical purpose or in a beneficial way.
31. *Various*: of different kinds or types; diverse
32. *Wonderful*: causing delight, pleasure, or admiration; excellent or marvelous

ADVERBS

1. *Nervously*: doing something with anxiety or tension; feeling uneasy or apprehensive
2. *Gently*: doing something in a delicate, mild, or tender manner
3. *Calmly*: doing something in a peaceful, tranquil, or composed manner; without agitation or disturbance
4. *Impurely*: doing something in a way that is not morally or ethically pure; with impurity or corruption
5. *Nervously*: doing something with anxiety or tension; feeling uneasy or apprehensive

A SOCIETY: ANSWERS

QUIZ (1)

1. The society began in a London teashop.
2. Everybody was talking about men while sitting around the open fire.
3. Polly's father was strange and very, very rich.
4. When Polly's father died, he left all of his money to her.
5. Polly had to read every book in the London Library to receive her inheritance
6. Every day for the past few months, Polly has gone to the London Library.
7. Polly couldn't bear to read another book because most of them were page after page of nonsense.
8. Polly thinks that Shakespeare's plays are excellent.

A SOCIETY: ANSWERS

9. (Answer may vary)
10. Polly thinks that Milton's poems are wonderful and Shelley's essays, fiction, and drama are superb.
11. Everybody said that the poetry Polly read must have been written by a woman or an amateur.
12. (Answer may vary)
13. Clorinda thinks that they are at fault for not spending time reading, despite being able to read.
14. They agreed to answer the question: Does society produce *good people* and *good books*?
15. They agreed not to enter into a relationship with a man or have a baby until they were satisfied that they had answered that question.

QUIZ (2)

1. Society members visited the British Museum, the King's Navy, Oxford University, Cambridge University, the Royal Academy

A SOCIETY: ANSWERS

of Arts, the Tate Gallery, concert halls, law courts, and theaters.

2. At each location they visited, they asked questions.
3. The members met at regular intervals and talked about what they had learned.
4. Rose went to the King's Navy. She dressed up as a North African prince.
5. The captain punished Rose to restore the honor of the King's Navy.
6. Rose asked the captain to hit her again to restore her honor.
7. The captain and Rose talked about Rose's family and childhood.
8. The captain and Rose promised to be best friends forever.
9. Fanny went to a court of law.
10. Fanny said that judges are not human but large animals trained to nod their heads and make sounds that nobody can understand.
11. On Fanny's second visit, she brought a bag full of flies.
12. She carried it into the court of law and opened it.

A SOCIETY: ANSWERS

13. Fanny fell asleep because the buzzing sound made by the flies was so pleasant.
14. When Fanny woke up, the prisoners were being led out of the courthouse.
15. The society members agreed that judges were not human, but rather animals.

QUIZ (3)

1. Helen went to the Royal Academy of Arts to learn about the paintings created by men.
2. Poems were in the blue book that Helen read.
3. (Answers may vary)
4. Helen described that the paintings by gesturing the size with her hands.
5. Castalia went to a university to find out if they produce *good people* and *good books*.
6. Castalia got into the professors' apartments and offices by dressing up as a cleaner.
7. (Answers may vary)
8. The professors' apartments and offices were filled from floor to ceiling with books and research papers.

9. Professor Hobkin and a professor from Germany wrote the book that Castalia read.
10. It was about an ancient Greek poet called Sappho.
11. (Answers may vary)
12. Castalia said that she would return to the university to find out if universities produce *good people* and *good books*.

QUIZ (4)

1. The narrator next saw Castalia three months later at a *society* meeting.
2. Everything about Castalia was beautiful; the way she walked, the expression on her face, and even her mood
3. Castalia had been to the university to find out if universities produce *good people* and *good books*.
4. Castalia said that answering the questions was so exciting, beautiful, and satisfying.
5. The *society* members agreed to stay pure until they understood what the world men had created was really like

A SOCIETY: ANSWERS

6. (Answers may vary)
7. Five years passed since the first *society* meeting.
8. The society members believed that labeling Castalia as impure was nonsense. (Answers may vary)
9. According to Polly, purity simply means a lack of knowledge and experience.
10. (Answers may vary)
11. Judith had been talking to scientists.
12. Judith wanted middle- and upper-class men to visit the special rooms in the underground.
13. Judith expected working-class women to work in the special rooms.
14. Judith expected middle- and upper-class women to visit the special rooms as customers.
15. Jane said that all the *society* members must now decide whether they still want to give birth.

QUIZ (5)

A SOCIETY: ANSWERS

1. The first two topics the *society* members discussed were science and engineering.
2. Three *society* members talked about those topics.
3. The members thought that man's achievements in those fields were far better than any of them had imagined.
4. (Answers may vary)
5. (Answers may vary)
6. (Answers may vary)
7. (Answers may vary)
8. (Answers may vary)
9. (Answers may vary)
10. Castalia looked unhappy because the questions they were asking had become too complex.
11. The members placed their answers to the complex questions they had been asking on a table in the middle of the room.
12. (Answers may vary)

QUIZ (6)

A SOCIETY: ANSWERS

1. Most men refused to talk about religion or what it meant to be good.
2. (Answers may vary)
3. Most men ignored the *society* members or became angry when asked about money or power.
4. The narrator thinks no one was attacked when asking these questions because men think that women are below them.
5. Many men think that women are inferior to them because they are influenced by societal beliefs propagated through the media.
6. The three famous women writers that Polly mentions are Jane Austen, Charlotte Brontë, and George Eliot.
7. Elizabeth had been researching literature.
8. She pretended to be a male editor to gain access to certain sources.
9. Elizabeth says that Mr. Arnold Bennett is the second most popular writer.
10. Elizabeth says that the five men write about real life.
11. Elizabeth believes that the truth has nothing to do with literature. (Answers vary)

A SOCIETY: ANSWERS

12. Jane was going to say, "Ladies, we must try to agree whether or no society produces *good people* and *good books*."
13. The men in the street shouting, "War! War! War! England is at war!"
14. The Prussians and the Austrians went to war over control of Germany.
15. (Answers may vary)

QUIZ (7)

1. A peace agreement was being discussed by Britain, Italy, France, and the US.
2. The narrator and Castalia were in the room where, before the war, they had held their *society* meetings.
3. The narrator felt it was strange how naïve they had been five years ago before the war.
4. The *society* members thought that the objective of life was to produce *good people* and *good books*.
5. The *society* members said that a good man must be honest, passionate, and interested

A SOCIETY: ANSWERS

in more than money, power, and goods. (Answers may vary)

6. A look of anger spread across Castalia's face because she thought that being able to read was the reason why they weren't happy with their lives.
7. Castalia thinks her mother was happy because she could not read.
8. Castalia tried to stop her daughter from reading.
9. Mr. Lloyd George was Britain's prime minister.
10. The narrator smiles ironically when she says that Castalia should try to make her daughter believe that men are more intelligent than women because she knows it's not true.
11. The narrator's name is Cassy.
12. (Answers may vary)
13. Castalia says that mothers have been helping their sons grow and learn for thousands of years.
14. Castalia says men need an innocent occupation, like giving birth and bringing up

children, in order for them to be *good people* and to write *good books*.
15. The narrator says that Castalia should teach her daughter, Ann, to believe in herself.

KEW GARDENS: VOCABULARY

NOUNS

1. *Candlestick*: a holder for a candle, typically made of metal or wood and often decorative in design
2. *Class*: class in society refers to a group of people who share similar economic and social status, typically determined by factors such as occupation, income, education level, and cultural background
3. *Colorful petals*: the brightly colored, often fragrant, outer parts of a flower that are typically used to attract pollinators
4. *Dragonfly*: an insect with long, slender body and four wings, usually brightly colored and found near water

5. ***Flour***: a finely ground powder made by grinding cereal grains or other starchy food sources
6. ***Flowerbed***: a plot of ground, often in a garden, where flowers are grown
7. ***Mermaid***: a mythical creature with the upper body of a human and the tail of a fish
8. ***Obstacles***: something that obstructs or hinders progress, such as a physical barrier or a difficult challenge
9. ***Orchid***: a type of flowering plant that typically has brightly colored and often fragrant blooms
10. ***Pagoda***: a tiered tower with multiple eaves, typically found in East Asia and often used as a religious structure
11. ***Palm tree***: a tall, tropical tree with a single straight trunk and large, fan-shaped leaves
12. ***Parasol***: a lightweight, often decorative umbrella used for protection from the sun
13. ***Roof***: the structure that covers the top of a building, typically made of materials such as shingles, tiles, or metal

KEW GARDENS: VOCABULARY

14. *Snail*: a small, slow-moving mollusk with a spiral shell and a soft, slimy body
15. *Snail shell*: the hard, spiral-shaped outer layer of a snail that serves as its protective covering
16. *Songbird*: a bird that is known for its musical ability, typically having a complex and melodious song
17. *Uruguay*: a country in South America known for its beaches, historic landmarks, and cultural heritage
18. *Waterlily*: a floating aquatic plant with large, circular leaves and brightly colored, often fragrant flowers

VERBS

1. *Approach*: approaches, approached, approaching - to move closer to something or someone in order to interact with it or them
2. *Crawl*: crawls, crawled, crawling - to move slowly on hands and knees or with the body close to the ground
3. *Contain*: contains, contained, containing -

to hold or have within a defined space, limit, or boundary

4. ***Disappear***: disappears, disappeared, disappearing - to cease to be visible or present
5. ***Dislike***: dislikes, disliked, disliking - to have a feeling of distaste or aversion toward someone or something
6. ***Experience***: experiences, experienced, experiencing - to have practical contact with and observation of events, situations, or people
7. ***Fly***: flies, flew, flying - to move through the air using wings or an engine
8. ***Follow***: follows, followed, following - to come or go after a person or thing proceeding ahead
9. ***Lead***: leads, led, leading - to guide or direct a group of people, an organization, or a process
10. ***Lean***: leans, leaned/leant, leaning - to rest against or be supported by something in a sloping position
11. ***Lose***: loses, lost, losing - to no longer have something or someone due to misplacing, failing to win or maintain, or death

KEW GARDENS: VOCABULARY

12. ***Press***: presses, pressed, pressing - to apply force to something in order to make it move or change shape
13. ***Rest***: rests, rested, resting - to cease from action or motion in order to relax or recover
14. ***Shake***: shakes, shook, shaken - to move back and forth or up and down with quick, short movements

ADJECTIVES

1. ***Eccentric***: unconventional or odd in behavior or appearance
2. ***Gentle***: having a mild and kind nature
3. ***Heart-shaped***: having a shape resembling the symbol for love
4. ***Impatient***: lacking patience or tolerance
5. ***Insignificant***: having little or no importance or meaning
6. ***Lower-middle class***: social class between the working class and middle class
7. ***Mad***: mentally unstable or crazy
8. ***Oval-shaped***: rounded and elongated
9. ***Random***: lacking a pattern or plan

KEW GARDENS: VOCABULARY

10. *Silent*: making no sound or noise
11. *Strange*: unfamiliar or unusual
12. *Upper-middle class*: social class between the middle and upper classes
13. *Opposite*: completely different or contrary
14. *Wonderful*: extremely good or enjoyable

ADVERBS

1. *Brightly*: emitting or reflecting a lot of light; shining with brightness
2. *Energetically*: with great energy, effort, or enthusiasm; vigorously or actively
3. *Luckily*: happening by chance or as a result of good fortune; fortunately
4. *Rapidly*: at a fast speed; happening quickly or without delay

KEW GARDENS: ANSWERS

QUIZ (1)

1. Kew Gardens is located in south-west London, and it contains gardens with plants from all over the world.
2. The oval-shaped flowerbed in Kew Gardens contains over a hundred flowers, each with heart-shaped leaves and colorful petals.
3. The man asked Lily to marry him while they were sitting by a lake in Kew Gardens, but Lily said "No".
4. The man imagined that if a dragonfly landed on Lily's foot, she would stop moving it and say "Yes" to his marriage proposal.
5. The man was walking with a woman named

KEW GARDENS: ANSWERS

Eleanor, and he asked her if she ever thinks about the past.
6. Eleanor remembers that it was from an old woman with gray hair and that it was the most wonderful kiss she had ever experienced.
7. The man, woman, and children walked away from the flowerbed together.

QUIZ (2)

1. The snail encountered obstacles such as blades of grass, stones, and dead leaves.
2. The insect left in the opposite direction.
3. The two men were an older man who claimed to hear the ghosts of dead people, and a younger man named William who was calm.
4. William showed the older man a beautiful flower in the flowerbed.
5. The older man claimed to have seen roses, nightingales, and mermaids in the forests of Uruguay, along with the most beautiful woman in Europe.

KEW GARDENS: ANSWERS

QUIZ (3)

1. The three people mentioned at the beginning of this chapter were two elderly women and an old man.
2. The elderly women weren't sure if the old man was eccentric or mad.
3. The elderly women were lower-middle class.
4. The elderly women were interested in the lives of the upper-middle class.
5. When the overweight woman stopped next to the oval-shaped flowerbed, she leaned over and looked at the flowers with curiosity, swayed backwards and forwards, ignoring the thin woman.
6. The overweight woman suggested going to have a cup of tea to the thin woman.

QUIZ (4)

1. The snail didn't want to climb over the leaf because it was too difficult, and it would take a long time to go around it.

KEW GARDENS: ANSWERS

2. A young couple on their first date approached the oval-shaped flowerbed.
3. The man said that on Fridays, they make you pay ten percent extra.
4. The couple talked about having tea brought to them as they sit at a white table among the gardens and him paying the bill.
5. Trissie was too excited to think about tea.
6. The man suggested Trissie follow him for tea.
7. Trissie saw beautiful orchids, cranes, wild flowers, a Chinese pagoda, and a bird with deep red-colored feathers on its head.
8. The voices of people and the beautiful colors of flowers filled the air at Kew Gardens.

NOTE FROM THE PUBLISHER

MATATABI PRESS is constantly seeking fresh talent. Contact us (Email: press@matatabi-japan.com) if you're:

- A writer who wishes to share their story with the world.
- An EFL/ESL professional who has a passion for creating English graded readers.
- A Japanese Language specialist who is interested in collaborating on a Japanese graded reader.
- A Japanese-English translator who is keen on translating any of our publications.

We welcome you to reach out to us and join our team.

NOTE FROM THE PUBLISHER

Matatabi Readers are graded by *sentence complexity* and *headword count*.

Sentence Complexity

Sentence Complexity Level	Flesch-Kincaid Grade Level
400	1 to 2
500	2 to 3
600	3 to 4
700	4 to 5
800	5 to 6
900	6 to 7
1000	7 to 8
1100	8 to 9
1200	9 to 10
1300+	10+

NOTE FROM THE PUBLISHER

The Flesch-Kincaid Grade Level Formula is used to calculate sentence complexity. For instance, Grade Level "3 to 4" (Level 600) means that the sentence complexity is appropriate for third and/or fourth-grade students in the U.S.

Headword Count

Headword Level	Headword Count
D	301 to 400
E	401 to 500
F	501 to 600
G	601 to 700
H	701 to 800
I	801 to 900
J	901 to 1000
K	1001 to 1100
L+	1101+

NOTE FROM THE PUBLISHER

The headword count in a Matatabi Reader indicates the number of words with distinct meanings. Regardless of the number of times a word is used in a book, it only counts as one headword. This applies to verbs, adjectives, and nouns, including all their forms. For instance:

- Eat, ate, eaten, and eating count as one headword.
- Tall, taller, and tallest count as one headword.
- Cake and cakes count as one headword.

NOTE FROM THE PUBLISHER

MATATABI TRANSLATION SERVICES
https://www.translate.matatabi-japan.com/

English Editing
(edit@matatabi-japan.com)
We provide editing services for various types of written materials, including essays, research articles, MA theses, doctoral theses, conference presentations, business emails, sound files, websites, and materials for publication.

Japanese-to-English Translation
(translate@matatabi-japan.com)
We offer translation services for various types of materials, including film subtitles/audiovisual translation (SRT, DFXP, SBV, SSA, TXT, VTT), business emails, essays, research articles, conference presentations, websites, picture books, and materials for publication.

EDITORS

Emily Aitken (Adaptor)

Emily is a highly experienced Japanese-English translator, with expertise in checking and proofreading. She currently resides in Edinburgh, Scotland, and has a specialization in audiovisual translation.

John McLean (Series Editor)

John is an accomplished associate professor at Yasuda Women's University in Hiroshima, Japan, where he oversees the Department of English Interpreting Stream. He is renowned for his outstanding translation and interpreting skills, which he has demonstrated in his work with prominent figures in the media, athletics, film, and entertainment industry.

www.ingramcontent.com/pod-product-compliance
Lightning Source LLC
Chambersburg PA
CBHW050256120526
44590CB00016B/2367